Yoga

calm Kids

By
William Anthony

BEARPORT PUBLISHING
Minneapolis, Minnesota

FUSION

Library of Congress Cataloging-in-Publication Data is available at www.loc.gov or upon request from the publisher.

ISBN: 978-1-64747-566-6 (hardcover)
ISBN: 978-1-64747-571-0 (paperback)
ISBN: 978-1-64747-576-5 (ebook)

This edition is published by arrangement with Booklife Publishing.

For more information, write to Bearport Publishing, 5357 Penn Avenue South, Minneapolis, MN 55419. Printed in the United States of America.

Photo Credits. All images courtesy of Shutterstock. With thanks to Getty Images, Thinkstock Photo, and iStockphoto. Recurring images: Abscent (pattern from cover), ag1100 (paper texture), Puslatronik (font), Sopelkin (doodle embellishments), Amy Li (illustrations and doodles). Cover - Nataliya Turpitko, p1 - Nataliya Turpitko, p2-3 - Patrick Foto, p4-5 - Rawpixel.com, Tom Wang, p6-7 - Africa Studio, GOLFX, p8-9 - wavebreakmedia, Ruslan Kalnitsky, p10-11 - Africa Studio, TinnaPong, p12-13 - Guntsoophack Yuktahnon, Rob Marmion, p14-15 - New Africa, aekkorn, p16-17 - Patrick Foto, p18-19 - Kasefoto, p20-21 - Ilike, Quintanilla, p22-23 - wavebreakmedia, Sakura Image Inc, Chutima Chaochaiya, Marharyta Gangalo

Contents

Healthy You

Keeping your body **healthy** can mean lots of things.
It can mean eating right, exercising, and getting good rest.

One very important part of staying healthy is taking care of your **mind**. Having a healthy mind helps us think clearly, make better decisions, and live better lives.

What Is Yoga?

Yoga helps you stretch your body and improve your balance.

Yoga exercises both the body and the mind. When you do yoga, you make shapes with your body.

People do yoga for lots of different reasons. It is a way to exercise your body. It helps you **focus** your mind.

Where Did Yoga Come From

Yoga is thought to be over 5,000 years old. It comes from India, which is a country in Asia.

Today, millions of people from all around the world do yoga. People do yoga on their own or in big groups.

Going to a class that has a teacher is a great way to try yoga.

Why Should I Do Yoga?

Yoga can do lots of good things for you. It is an exercise that can make you stronger. It can help you stretch better. It can also help your balance.

Yoga can help you feel calmer. It can also help you lower your **stress** and think more clearly.

Yoga makes you focus on what your body is doing.

Breathing

Breathing is an important part of yoga. During yoga, we notice each breath in and out. It helps you focus.

Poses

Yoga **poses** are the shapes we make with our bodies during yoga. Each pose has a special name.

Lotus Pose

Are you ready to try some yoga poses? Let's start with lotus pose.

1 Sit on the floor with your back straight.

2 Cross your legs.

3 Bring your hands toward your knees and hold them like this.

4 Close your eyes, and take some deep breaths in and out. Focus on every breath.

Yoga may be harder to do on some days than on others. That's okay!

Tree Pose

Now, let's try tree pose.

1 Stand up straight.

2 Picture one of your feet as planted into the ground. Put your other foot on top of it.

3 Bring your hands together above your head.

4 Slowly bring your foot that is not planted up higher. Make sure it is above or below your knee, never on it!

5 Breathe deeply.

6 Try the pose again with your other leg.

Cat and Cow Poses

Use cat pose and cow pose together. Let's try it!

1. Kneel down and place your hands on the floor in front of you as wide as your shoulders.
2. Look down at the floor.
3. Arch your back up like an angry cat.

Cat Pose

4 Slowly drop your tummy toward the floor like a cow.

5 Bring your head up and look forward.

6 As you move into cow pose, breathe in. As you move into cat pose, breathe out.

Cow Pose

Yoga Can Do What?

Doing yoga can make amazing things happen. Some people think yoga can help you sleep better.

Others say yoga could even keep you from getting sick.

Calm Kids

Yoga is a very good way to keep our minds healthy and calm. If yoga doesn't work for you, that's okay! There are other ways to take care of yourself.

Try these things!

Mindfulness

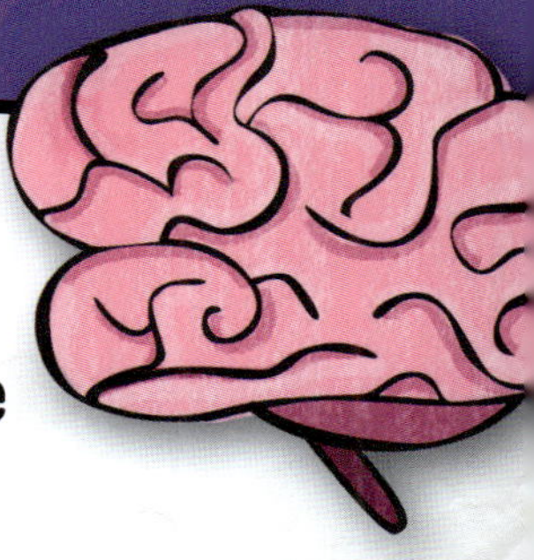

Being mindful helps you notice things around you.

Meditation

Meditation goes well with yoga! It can help you think about your feelings.

Self-Care

Self-care means taking care of yourself.

Glossary

balance	the ability to move or to stay in one place without losing control or falling
focus	to give your full attention to something
healthy	when the body and mind are working at their best
improve	make better
mind	the part of a person that thinks, feels emotions, and remembers
poses	the shapes you make with your body during yoga
stress	something that causes strong feelings of worry

Index